Sloths/Perezosos

By Julie Guidone

Reading Consultant: Susan Nations, M.Ed.,
author/literacy coach/consultant in literacy development

WEEKLY READER®
PUBLISHING

Please visit our web site at **www.garethstevens.com**.
For a free catalog describing our list of high-quality books,
call 1-800-542-2595 (USA) or 1-800-387-3178 (Canada).
Our fax: 1-877-542-2596

Library of Congress Cataloging-in-Publication Data

Guidone, Julie.
  (Sloths. Spanish & English)
  Sloths / by Julie Guidone / Perezosos / por Julie Guidone.
    p. cm. — (Animals that live in the rain forest / Animales de la selva)
  Includes bibliographical references and index.
  ISBN-10: 1-4339-0065-3 ISBN-13: 978-1-4339-0065-5 (lib. bdg.)
  ISBN-10: 1-4339-0115-3 ISBN-13: 978-1-4339-0115-7 (softcover)
  1. Sloths—Juvenile literature. I. Title. II. Title: Perezosos.
 QL737.E2G8518 2009
 599.3'13—dc22   2008040232

This edition first published in 2009 by
Weekly Reader® Books
An Imprint of Gareth Stevens Publishing
1 Reader's Digest Road
Pleasantville, NY 10570-7000 USA

Copyright © 2009 by Gareth Stevens, Inc.

Executive Managing Editor: Lisa M. Herrington
Senior Editor: Barbara Bakowski
Creative Director: Lisa Donovan
Designers: Michelle Castro, Alexandria Davis
Photo Researcher: Diane Laska-Swanke
Publisher: Keith Garton
Translation: Tatiana Acosta and Guillermo Gutiérrez

Photo Credits: Cover © Buddy Mays/Corbis; pp. 1, 7, 9, 13, 19 © Michael & Patricia Fogden/Minden
Pictures; p. 5 © Michael & Patricia Fogden/CORBIS; p. 11 © Donald Enright/Alamy; p. 15 © Gerry Ellis/
Minden Pictures; p. 17 © Tui De Roy/Minden Pictures; p. 21 (both) © Ingo Arndt/Foto Natura/
Minden Pictures

Printed in the United States of America

1 2 3 4 5 6 7 8 9 10 09 08

Table of Contents

- - - - - - - - - - - -

Contenido

Boldface words appear in the glossary./
Las palabras en **negrita** aparecen en el glosario.

An Upside-Down Life

Sloths are animals that live in the **rain forest**. Rain forests are warm, wet woodlands. Sloths spend most of their lives hanging upside down in trees.

- - - - - - - - - - - - - -

Una vida cabeza abajo

Los perezosos son animales que viven en la **selva tropical**. Las selvas tropicales son bosques cálidos y húmedos. Los perezosos pasan la mayor parte de su vida colgados de los árboles cabeza abajo.

Sloths sleep and eat upside down. They even have their babies in trees. A baby sloth rides along on its mother's stomach.

- - - - - - - - - - - - -

Los perezosos comen y duermen cabeza abajo. Estos animales hasta tienen a sus crías subidos en los árboles. La cría de perezoso va agarrada a la panza de su madre.

baby sloth/
cría de perezoso

A sloth is about the size of a large cat. It has long legs and curved **claws**. The claws help the sloth hold on to tree branches.

– – – – – – – – – – – – – –

Un perezoso tiene un tamaño similar al de un gato grande. Tiene las patas largas y unas **garras** curvas que lo ayudan a sujetarse a las ramas de los árboles.

claws/
garras

9

Leafy Greens

Sloths like to eat leaves. They use their hard lips to bite the leaves. They crush the leaves with teeth in their cheeks.

- - - - - - - - - - - - - -

Hojas verdes

A los perezosos les gusta comer hojas. Primero, muerden las hojas con sus duros labios. Después, las trituran con los dientes de los carrillos.

Leaves do not give a sloth much energy.
The sloth moves slowly. It falls asleep
upside down with its head tucked
close to its body.

— — — — — — — — — — — — — —

Como las hojas no les dan mucha
energía, los perezosos se mueven
con gran lentitud. Se quedan dormidos
colgados con la cabeza recogida
cerca del cuerpo.

Staying Safe

A sloth's long gray-brown hair blends in with the trees. Other animals cannot see the sloth.

- - - - - - - - - - - - - -

Evitar el peligro

El largo pelaje gris pardo de los perezosos se confunde con el color de los árboles. Por eso, otros animales no notan su presencia.

hair/
pelaje

Sloths use their sharp claws to fight off **predators**. Large snakes, harpy eagles, and **jaguars** hunt sloths.

- - - - - - - - - - - - - -

Los perezosos usan sus afiladas garras para defenderse de los **depredadores**. Animales como las serpientes grandes, las águilas harpía y los **jaguares** cazan perezosos.

harpy eagle/
águila harpía

Most predators live on the ground,
so sloths stay safe in the trees.
On land, they can only crawl slowly.
In water, sloths swim very well!

- - - - - - - - - - - - - -

Como la mayoría de sus
depredadores viven en el suelo,
los perezosos se sienten más
seguros en los árboles. En tierra, los
perezosos sólo pueden arrastrarse
muy lentamente. Sin embargo, ¡en
el agua nadan muy bien!

How Many Toes?

All sloths have three toes on their back legs. Two-toed sloths have two toes on their front legs. How many toes do three-toed sloths have on their front legs?

- - - - - - - - - - - - - -

¿Cuántos dedos?

Todos los perezosos tienen tres dedos en las patas traseras. Los perezosos de dos dedos tienen dos dedos en las patas delanteras. ¿Cuántos dedos tienen en las patas delanteras los perezosos de tres dedos?

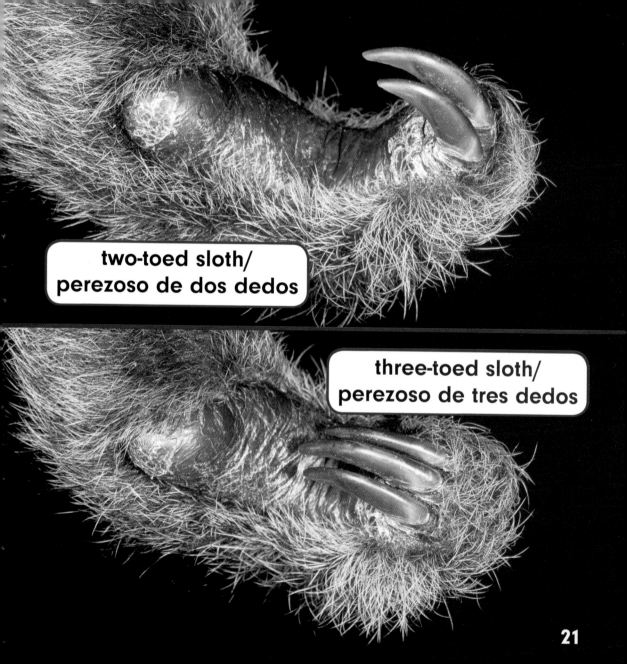

two-toed sloth/
perezoso de dos dedos

three-toed sloth/
perezoso de tres dedos

Glossary/Glosario

claws: sharp, hooked nails on an animal's foot

jaguars: big cats that live in rain forests

predators: animals that kill and eat other animals

rain forest: a warm, rainy woodland with many types of plants and animals

- - - - - - - - - - - - - - - - - - -

depredadores: animales que matan a otros animales para comérselos

garras: uñas ganchudas y afiladas de los animales

jaguares: felinos de gran tamaño que viven en la selva tropical

selva tropical: bosque cálido y húmedo donde viven muchos tipos de animales y plantas

For More Information/Más información

Books/Libros

On the Banks of the Amazon/En las orillas del Amazonas. Nancy Kelly Allen (Raven Tree Press, 2004)

The Sloth: World's Slowest Animal/El perezoso: El mamífero más lento del mundo. Record-Breaking Animals/Campeones del mundo animal (series). Joy Paige (Rosen Publishing, 2004)

Web Sites/Páginas web

Enchanted Learning: Sloths/Perezosos
www.enchantedlearning.com/subjects/mammals/sloth
Learn more about sloths, and print a picture to color./ Aprendan más datos sobre los perezosos e impriman un dibujo para colorear.

New York Zoos and Aquarium: Sloth Video/ Zoológicos y acuarios de Nueva York: Video de un perezoso
nyzoosandaquarium.com/cpz_news/twotoedsloth
Watch Matilda, a two-toed sloth, on the move at the Central Park Zoo./Observen en movimiento a Matilda, un perezoso de dos dedos del zoológico de Central Park.

Index/Índice

About the Author

Julie Guidone has taught kindergarten and first and second grades in Madison, Connecticut, and Fayetteville, New York. She loves to take her students on field trips to the zoo to learn about all kinds of animals! She lives in Syracuse, New York, with her husband, Chris, and her son, Anthony.

- - - - - - - - - - - - - -

Información sobre la autora

Julie Guidone ha sido maestra de jardín de infancia, y de primero y segundo grado en Madison, Connecticut, y en Fayetteville, Nueva York. ¡A Julie le encanta ir de excursión al zoológico con sus alumnos para que conozcan todo tipo de animales! Julie vive en Syracuse, Nueva York, con su esposo Chris y su hijo Anthony.